Lilbit

(A Grandmother's Love Transcends)

Mary E. Gilder

Copyright © 2025 by Mary E. Gilder

All rights reserved. Without limiting the right of copyright reserved above, no part of this book may be reproduced, stored in a retrieval system or transmitted in any form or by any means without the prior written permission of the authors—except by a reviewer who may quote brief passages in a review to be printed in a newspaper, magazine or journal.

Published by
MEG's Publishing
3139 W. Holcombe Boulevard, #750
Houston, Texas 77025

This is a work of non-fiction.

Book Cover and Interior Designed by:
Jessica Tilles, jessica@twasolutions.com

ISBN: 978-0-9823844-2-8 (paperback)
ISBN: 978-0-9823844-3-5 (hardcover)

Library of Congress Control Number: 2025900258

Books are available at quatity discounts. For information, contact the publisher.

Distributed by Ingram Content Group
www.ingramcontent.com

Acknowledgments

HARPO Producer, Jessica Dres: Much appreciation is extended to you for reaching out and honoring my journey and ability to inspire.

Red Book Magazine: Your interview challenged me to connect with the trauma I endured following Lilbit's passing. Thank you for highlighting and celebrating my evolution and its impact on humanity.

Northern California Museum and Library: Thank you for cataloging *A Misrepresentation of Myself* and *Even a Man Can Have a Broken Heart*. Your support has profoundly touched me.

Houston's Ensemble Theater: Your yearly support and production of the *Even a Man Panel* was the catalyst for the *Even a Man* documentary.

The Gilder Family (Rayford, Torry, Tiera and Marshana): In 2017, when I could not remember my words, you reminded me of the importance of standing in bravery and that God has the final say. Thank you.

To **My Mother** Yvonne: You, my dear, have been my biggest literary encourager, pitching my novels to anyone who would give you a few minutes of their time. Thank you for trusting in my earthly assignment and for loving what my mind creates. I must also acknowledge and thank you for allowing Lilbit and me to spend countless hours together.

Had it not been for your obedience, this assignment would not have been fulfilled. She and I needed time to build and cement our bond. Love you, "Snagg."

To **My Godmother** Bettye: Thank you for your endless support and encouragement.

I Am Woman, Hear Me ROAR: To my goddaughters—Jeanette, Cherina, Zahava, and Airiel—continue to be bold, brave, courageous, brilliant, sassy, and classy. You are only here for a moment; cower down to no one.

The Phenomenal Literary Assistants: Airiel, Nichole, and Kirsten, you make me look "damn good."

To **My Brilliant Editor** Jessica Tilles: Thank you, thank you, thank you!

Appreciation Extended to **My Literary Mentors**: author/filmmaker Renay Jackson and publicist/author/columnist Cyrus Webb.

Everyone Needs "Literary Partners in Crime": author and playwright Sheryl Mallory Johnson, you are that and so much more. Authors and filmmakers Marshana Gilder and Tiera Cornish, you sassy literary gurus are the bomb diggity.

Lifetime Mentors: Thank you for feeding my soul with your wisdom: Dr. Patricia Oyeshiku, Dr. Quindola Crowley, Dr. Susan Sanfillipo, and Judge Rhonda Burges.

Much **Appreciation Extended To**: Dr. John J. Volpi, Dr. Mansayac, Dr. Gloria Carreon, Dr. Ash Jain, and Dr. Grace Seijo—your compassion and compliance with your earthly assignments have blessed humanity.

I Could Not Go Without Mentioning Memorial Hermann-TIRR **Medical Teams**: Moursond, Kirby Glen, and Sugarland, TX—you inspire and provide hope 24/7. Never forget that truth. Love you all.

To My Loving Family and **Awesome Friends Who Are Also Family**: Thank you for loving me as you do. I take nothing for granted, especially kindness, compassion, and loyalty.

Auntie Debra Norris: My ten-year-old self recalls you being Lilbit's "right-hand girl." Your impact is engraved in my heart. A big thank you from me and my siblings.

In Dedication

This remarkable, powerful, and phenomenal book is dedicated to the descendants of Mary Elizabeth Conley: I believe that she knew her earthly journey would conclude abruptly. I would like to think she understood that the writing of this book would be one of my earthly assignments. She gifted me all the lessons needed to gift them to you. Through me, my first and second cousins who made their earthly arrivals following her passing, can embrace the essence of her love, the depth of her passion, her commitment to her family, and her love for humanity.

In Dedication

To my grandchild, Anthony Rejiv Cornish Jr. As soon as I picked up my pen to author Lilbit's journey, I found out I was going to be a nanna. I will share Lilbit's lessons and rituals with you, my precious grandson.

In Dedication

Last but not least, to my soul mate, Mary Elizebeth Conley (Lilbit): ***Your Lessons and Rituals Have Transcended.***

Grace Mandolas love continues to transcend

My maternal grandmother, Grace Mandola, taught me the most. She taught me the value of the family meal. She was the best cook that I have ever met and she said that the most important ingredient was to cook with a lot of love.

Grace Mandola was selfless and showed us unconditional love through her mastery of exquisite food. She didn't preach to us; she led through her actions. I have an MBA and it did not come from an IVY League Education, it came from my Maw Maw.

—Johnny Carrabba III, Founder of
Johnny Carrabba-Family of Restaurants
(Carrabba's, Graces and Mia's)

TABLE OF CONTENTS

Introduction xix
Prologue 1
Chapter 1: The Pink House 11
Chapter 2: Rituals 17
Chapter 3: Courageous Spirit 29
Chapter 4: Unspoken Understanding 35
Chapter 5: Gifted the Lessons by Her Actions 41
Chapter 6: Her Challenges 49
Chapter 7: Religious Foundation 55
Chapter 8: The Embracement of Her Name—
　　　　　Go Figure 61
Chapter 9: My Badge of Shame 67
Chapter 10: The Birth of a Shift 75
Chapter 11: Change 83
Chapter 12: Traumatized (Inner Bully) 89
Chapter 13: Metamorphosis (Outside-In) 99
Chapter 14: Time Brings About Change 105
Chapter 15: A Grandmother's Love Transcends 111
Greatest Lesson Gifted by Your Grandmother 113

What Your Grandmother Meant to You 119
Discussion Questions 131
Word of Hello 133
About the Author 134
My Heroes 137
I Was Never Alone: A Tribute of Thanks 138
Closing Message 143

God's Timing

For several years, my readers have asked, "Mary, why has it been nine years since your last literary release?" My response is always, "I write when God issues my next assignment. I will pick up my pen when He states it's time."

To my readers, enjoy the fruits of my patience and compliance.

– Mary Elizabeth Gilder (MEG)

INTRODUCTION

I continuously state that love is the foundation and there is no greater investment. The respect and love I hold within my life began with Lilbit. She was my everything. Did I mention she was my everything? The level of empathy and compassion I exude was birthed from our relationship. She was my soulmate, my confidant, my protector, and my shero. You see, Lilbit was my maternal grandmother. Forty-seven years following her earthly departure, her gifted lessons have transcended. Her powerful lessons have not only blessed my life but have blessed my children's journeys as well. As I celebrate her rich legacy, and the lessons she gifted to me, I celebrate all grandmothers. I embrace the love, the rituals, and the numerous lessons they have bestowed. Lessons that transcend from one generation to the next generation.

In honoring Lilbit and her unforgettable journey, this beautiful book honors all referred to as Nanna, Momma, Big Momma, Grandmother, Granny, Grams, Gramma, Grammie, Glamma, Memaw, Nanny, Abuela, Nona, Lola, Baba, Queen, Bibi, Babushka, Gam Gam, YaYa, Ouma, Nai Nai, GiGi, Geema, Vovo, Obaasan, Savta, Tatik, and Tutu…the list goes on and on.

Prologue

The year was 1970. It was Saturday morning, and I was beyond excited. I had made my bed, Mrs. Beasley sat next to my pillows, my collection of books sat on my bookshelf, toys tucked away in the oak toy box, I had unplugged the baby blue and white cake batter-stained Easy Bake Oven, and I had finally organized my closet. I swiftly finished my bowl of Malt-O-Meal, devoured a slice of raisin bread, and gulped down a glass of orange juice. Dressed to impress, I wore my

Saturday best. My hair sported its usual mess, but I didn't care as I headed to the most exciting place on Earth.

"Bye, Mom. I will be back after cartoons."

Oh, how I loved my Saturday morning ritual: *The Flintstones*, *The Jetsons*, *Underdog*, *The Pink Panther*, *Yogi Bear*, and *Bugs Bunny*.

"Okay. Be careful. Tell everyone I said hello."

I sat on my emerald-green bike, eagerly preparing to head to the Pepto Bismol pink house nestled in the middle of the crowded cul-de-sac. I backed my green machine out of the driveway, turned, and waved across the street to the feisty twins, Kayla and Shayla, my "bestest" friends when we weren't at odds. We fought every other day. One day I fought with Kayla and days later, Shayla. On rare occasions, I fought with both simultaneously. My older brother, Richard, declared me the victor all the time. Between the fighting, we played tag, dodge ball, red light-green light, and jacks, and ate Twinkies, Moon Pies, chips, dill pickles, candy, and played with our dolls.

Directly next door to our sage house with the white picket fence lived our friend, Kevin. Along with being nice, he enjoyed building go-carts, tree houses, riding bikes, and playing baseball with Richard. Kevin grew up to become a famous MVP baseball player.

As I journeyed up the street, I glanced at the tan house to my left; a busy house with daily yelling, cursing, fighting, straight out beat downs. The police visited the property more than their relatives did . The mother constantly threatened to put the father out. That's what I recall my family saying. For some unbeknownst reason, they assumed I did not understand their conversations.

As I pedaled faster toward my heart's desire, I approached the lovely white house to my right with the dark red door. I spent a lot of time at that white house with my classmate and her family, who were from Mexico City. They resided in the most beautiful home. Their whimsical, picture-perfect hunter-green lawn hosted perfectly landscaped flower beds, plants, and trees. A man-made pond positioned in the center of the front yard provided entertainment for the squalling ducks and geese. According to rumors, the parents spoiled their children. During my many visits, they extended that spoiling to me. The hospitality ended with the family dog, a black and white villain with an axe to grind with the green machine that would chase me further up the street until being redirected.

Across from the white house was Juan's house. Richard and Juan were friends. Juan's family home was built on a lot that had been empty for years. Their home stood out because it was a "new build" and it was "fancy." Grandpa said something about Juan's father having a successful construction company in Tijuana Mexico. Their youngest sibling was the youngest of twelve and she was my buddy.

I loved visiting their festive family home, spending the night and devouring her mother's delicious cuisine: homemade tortillas, menudo, tamales, beef tacos, rice, and pinto beans. As I journeyed further, my heart plunged to my feet, and I used my sleeve to remove the sweat streaming down my forehead. The light cream house with the thorny red rose bushes became less of a blur as I dodged away from the approaching car and the penetrating glare coming from the driver as her bronze Oldsmobile whisked through the awaiting silver gates. She swiftly exited as her bony legs dashed toward the front door. My knees buckled as I glanced at the cat eyeglasses nestled on the tip of her pointy nose, staring in the direction of the playing children. The frame of her metal screen door rattled as she slithered in. That was that until our next creepy encounter.

The heels of my black tennis shoes dug into the dirt as the green machine came to a screeching halt. I took a deep breath as the sweet scent of jasmine, gardenia, and various roses captivated my senses. I had made it. I had arrived. I was in heaven—my heaven, my refuge, my place of solitude. My arrival represented my reconnection with the foundation of love's manifestation in my life. Yes, I had arrived. Let the fun begin.

"Grandmother, I'm here!"

"There are numerous stories to be written about this remarkable woman... this is the one she gifted to me."

—*Mary Elizabeth Gilder*

Chapter 1
"The Pink House"

Chapter 1

Before age ten, I had joy in my life, and I knew I was loved. However, my introduction with profound love came from my grandmother, Mary Elizabeth, affectionately known as Lilbit. I bear her name and a strong resemblance. As a small child, I spent hours at the pink house. We lived on the same street and frequently, I would tell my mom, "I'm going to Grandmother's for a visit," and would not return home for several days.

Lilbit had a drawer in her hallway that smelled of mothballs. It housed clothing and toiletries purchased for her grandchildren. At bedtime, after I took a bath, she rubbed pink Johnson's baby lotion on me and then sprinkled baby powder all over my body. Then, she smeared Vaseline on my lips, gave me Dristan nose drops to address my allergies, and cough medicine just in case a sneeze, cough, or squeal presented itself. She transformed the living room sofa into a bed, lay me down, tucked me in while pulling the covers up to my neck, and plastered a big kiss on my cheek. I loved her kisses. The television entertained Grandpa as he watched *Gunsmoke, Rifleman, Bonanza*, or *The Wild Wild West* as I drifted off to sleep. The next morning, I always felt rejuvenated.

Lilbit was an enormous support. One of the many ways she supported my mother was by ensuring that I celebrated my birthdays with my classmates. One year, she arrived at my pre-kindergarten classroom with balloons, a large vanilla cake covered with pink and white roses, ice cream, and punch, and looked her finest. With her wavy, jet-black hair pulled back in a bun, she wore a simple dress with white tennis shoes. She applied her signature apple red lipstick to her lips and continuously popped her favorite chewing gum. This scenario played out for several years. I never forgot how Lilbit showed up for me.

Lilbit was an excellent cook. I know that to be true because I was her shadow. At this very moment, as I close my eyes, I visualize myself in her kitchen, sitting at the square table, watching her every move as she sliced, diced, chopped, boiled, sauteed, and fried. My eyes recorded every detail and my mind locked into every memory. Many of her recipes I prepare for my family. A few of my favorite dishes include mustard greens/turnips/okra, chop suey, coleslaw, carrot salad, fried chicken, roasted pork chops, and spaghetti.

Lilbit's table sat four. She, Grandpa, and my two aunts lived in the home. I'm unsure where they all ate, as she reserved the kitchen table for her three grandbabies. She instructed my youngest aunt to place a pillow on each of the chairs and a large towel would cover the pillows. Regardless of our stature, she ordered us to sit on the pillows. After she placed a large paper towel above our shirt collars, she served us a plate of deliciousness. I savored every bite. Every bite was mouthwatering good—the flavors, textures, and aromas are forever locked in my memory. I don't recall dessert being a grand event, but I have a feeling that Lilbit prided herself on presenting Carnation ice cream or her famous strawberry Jell-O with fruit cocktail, which she loved.

Chapter 2
"Rituals"

A series of actions that you perform regularly. Rituals are meaningful acts you do with intent. Rituals embody what matters to you by putting your values into practice.

Chapter 2

Ritual One: My Lunch Date

In kindergarten, Lilbit picked me up from school most days at noon. Upon returning to her home, she would put on her colorful apron and prepare lunch, which was the usual peanut butter sandwich, two inches thick, with the peanut butter sticking to the roof of my mouth, and beef bologna and cheese served with mustard on Wonder Bread. Lilbit would serve Mother's cookies—brown cookies with yellow frosting in the middle. These cookies failed to excite my senses, but Lilbit deemed them the perfect compliment. Lays potato chips (no one can eat just one), a tall glass of cold milk, a large red apple or an orange.

My daily lunch experience also included catching up on Ms. Liz Foster and her three children: Snapper, Greg, and Jill, as well as Mrs. Chancellor, her son Brock, and Victor and Nikki Newman from *The Young and the Restless*. I was only six years of age, but I understood Jill was in love with Mrs. Chancellor's husband, and this had Mrs. Chancellor upset. Following that show, *General Hospital*, *The Guiding Light*, *Days of Our Lives*, and *As the World Turns* entertained us. Lilbit and I sat in silence as I learned from her and the ABC Television Network an appreciation for the writers of daytime television.

Ritual Two: Her Apprentice

Lilbit was a caring woman who was involved with her church and her community. Many of the individuals in her life were much older. For many years, she worked as a domestic, cleaning the homes of San Diego's elite—older, privileged white women living in North Park and Golden Hills in the late 1960s. I accompanied her to the residences.

During these visits, she instructed me to sit quietly, watch television, and not touch anything. I complied as I sat in amazement, observing the beautiful artwork, furnishings, vases, and whatnots. One client, Mrs. McIntosh, referred to me as "darling" and gifted me candy, soda, chips, and hugs. "Hello, darling," or "Good morning, darling, would you like a piece of candy, darling?" I loved going to her home, the fancy Victorian in Golden Hills.

Ritual Three: Her Plus One

Another ritual thrust upon me was attending viewings. How did I become her plus one? I recall on a day that felt pretty familiar, Lilbit stated that a dear friend of hers had passed away and she and I were going to view her body. This ritual occurred time after time. I'm unsure why Lilbit concluded that this was appropriate. I was scared to death of death.

On one occasion, the viewing was in the family's living room. When I entered the small home, there was laughter, guests indulging in food, and playing cards as the mounted casket was center stage in the living room. I will never forget that dreadful image and the impact it left on me. Lilbit strutted in with her trademark pound cake, hugged several people, and introduced me as she paid her respects. She wore a beautiful dress, white tennis shoes, hair in a bun, and her signature apple red lipstick, a vision of beauty.

My young self sat in silence, trying to ascertain the importance of my presence. "Why am I here?" Lilbet housed no confusion. We were peanut butter and jelly and, in her soul, dwelled on an understanding of that truth. Discomfort plagued me for years and perhaps is the reason for my held affliction with death, viewings, and funerals.

Ritual Four: Saturday Busyness

Saturdays at Lilbit's were full of busyness. The mornings would start early, with her preparing the expected feast, which was rarely any surprises: smoked bacon that was at least two inches in thickness, eggs sunny side up, and biscuits light on top, crispy on the bottom, and dripping in Carnation butter. She loved strawberry preserves, as did her grandbabies. She served the Carnation milk ice cold. I don't recall children's plates. We received our meals on standard-size plates. There were no rules about not being dismissed until we ate every morsel. My two siblings and I gladly consumed the deliciousness referred to as breakfast, lunch, and dinner.

I must mention the white oven. That oven was something pretty special. It had four eyes, with a griddle in the middle. From time to time, Lilbit used the griddle to prepare pancakes or French toast. The oven front had three doors: the top right for baking, the bottom right was for broiling, and the left side was for storing pots, skillets, and pans. I was amazed by its beauty and mastery. On occasion, I see modern replicas displayed in magazines. The sight always brings my thoughts to my grandmother's large kitchen that she managed like an HGTV cooking show. When Lilbit put on her apron and washed her hands, that was my signal to assume my position at the kitchen table, watching and processing her every move. There was little conversation between us as she moved in silence. Yet, each slice, chop, dice, and stir presented me with a rich culinary experience.

Before I drifted, I was speaking about her Saturday rituals. Following Saturday morning breakfast, Aunt Debra ensured we were dressed and prepared for outside fun. I played indoor and outdoor games or watched television as I eagerly awaited my Saturday favorites, which included drama with the twins. At some point, Grandpa would take over the television to watch his westerns. Most Saturday afternoons would end with some horror movie like *Dracula, The Birds, Night of the Living Dead, Frankenstein,* or *Godzilla.* That creepy list clearly explains my fear of scary movies.

Ritual Five: The Market

It was great being a child during this time; life was beyond good. I played outside, journeying between my home and Lilbit's home, using the green machine, my skates, or my legs as my mode of transportation. Often Lilbit and I would go to her favorite grocery store: Sawaya Brothers, which was equivalent to attending a Latin festival. The store's interior burst with fluorescent colors as festive music filled the air, awakening my young soul with its energy. I was moving and grooving as Lilbit walked up and down each aisle, popping her chewing gum as she surveyed her options. She was a creature of habit, purchasing the same items. What I enjoyed most about our shopping trip was her time spent with the butchers in their white attire, each addressing her as Ms. Conley as she perused the strategically displayed varieties of beef, pork, poultry, fish, and cold cuts before she requested her usual selections: pork chops, ground beef, chicken, fish, and thick smoked bacon, all packaged to her satisfaction in white butcher paper. I found myself intrigued by the large display of dill pickles and pig feet on the countertop. I looked forward to my crunchy dill pickle as a reward for being obedient. The taste of dill pickles continues to remind me of my time shared with Lilbit at the market. During my visits to San Diego, I drive to our shopping spot, park my car, and reminisce.

Ritual Six: Making Room For All

Lilbit's home appeared massive, when in fact it was a two-bedroom, one-bath ranch style. She had converted the garage into an entertainment room. During my childhood, the home housed my grandmother, my grandpa, and two of my three aunts. I always felt there was plenty of space. I never felt restricted by the home's square footage.

One afternoon, which reflected so many, we were watching television around 8:00 p.m. when a flash of light peered in through the living room blinds. Lilbit eagerly opened the front door. Instantly, enthusiasm filled the room as voices yelled, "It's Uncle Leroy and Aunt Ula!" The caramel Cadillac, stuffed to capacity, slowly pulled into the driveway. Each strutted in wearing their best threads: suits, Stacy Adams, hats, dresses, high heels, and the finale, Lilbit's baby sister, sexy Aunt Thelma, with her long legs, curvaceous hips, frosted lipstick, blonde hair, and long lashes. She was a vision of perfection.

Our Los Angeles family had arrived; never providing advanced warning—Lilbit's words. They placed pallets on the carpet and used both sofas. That is simply what Lilbit did. The unannounced visits always appeared to be welcomed and embraced.

I inherited that ideology. In my early years of marriage, we made room for all. Also, when visiting family or friends, I'm content with a blanket and pillow. I will find a spot and be perfectly content. Uncle Leroy and Aunt Ula's visits were always short. Twenty-four hours, to be exact, of so much joy and laughter.

The next morning, Lilbit prepared dark-roasted Folgers coffee and a hearty breakfast before their departure. After everyone gathered at the front door, they exchanged hugs, kisses, and reassurances of future unannounced visits. Then they piled into the sleek Cadillac and headed towards Highway 805 North.

Ritual Seven: No One Departed Empty-Handed

Lilbit mastered the practice of gifting tokens of love to her guests. No one departed from her home empty-handed. Most guests just showed up without an invitation—the entire family: Dad, Mom, and the children. Lilbit always made all who entered her home feel welcome. Especially her family members. That was typical in the late sixties and seventies. If there was food available, you ate. You could not depart from her home without a piece of fruit, cookies, cake, pie, chewing gum, or candy. It was her way of sharing with you a piece of herself. It was her gesture of love and appreciation that you set aside time out of your day to pay her family a visit. On one memorable occasion, a family member visited with his wife and small children. Lilbit made it a priority to ensure everyone felt welcomed. After what I perceived as a lengthy visit, and after bundling up the children in coats, scarves, and gloves, Lilbit gave each a pack of Juicy Fruit gum and a roll of multicolored Life Savers before they left. For several years, I observed this ritual unfold. I'm unsure when I became cognizant of how many lives would be impacted because of my knowledge and embracement of this ritual.

Chapter 3
"Courageous Spirit"

Chapter 3

Grandmother's nickname was Lilbit. I'm assuming she was bestowed the name due to her short stature. She stood an even five-foot-four inches. However small, her frame housed a giant personality. Lilbit, a gum poppin' pistol, rarely allowed herself to be intimidated and fearlessly followed through on every threat, promise, or vow she made.

On one occasion, my mother, who was newly married, was in a heated argument with my stepfather. When Lilbit got wind of the situation, she marched up Gregory Street. The subtleness glistening from the streetlights guided each stride. The heaviness of the large oak door caused an unwelcoming introduction as it granted her entrance. She barged in like the po po, while demanding a response to her list of inquiries. I can't recall the words provided. However, Lilbit spoke her truth, made her demands, and the foolishness ceased. From the view my bedroom wall vent provided, her boldness as she strutted away from the massive door and proceeded south captivated me. I imagine the gleaming moonlight provided a view of the twin's massive house. Lilbit knew I loved that yellow house. She quickly swayed her hips as she passed by Kevin's house. I'm sure she glanced at the "business" to her left, perhaps wondering if her officiating skills were of need. I'm sure as she increased her strides, admiration filled her senses as she marveled over the whimsical white house with the dark red door and contemplated how she could incorporate a few of their decorative contributions. I'm certain she waved at Juan's parents as they sat outside. Late evenings provided them an opportunity to sit on their front porch as they listened to Latin music and engaged in conversion. Lilbit held their family in high regard. Unfortunately, she did not extend the same sentiments to Mrs. Cat Eyes. Unlike me,

Lilbit's knees did not buckle, nor did sweat flee from her face and there was not an acceleration of her beating heart. She welcomed a verbal rumble with the neighborhood bully. She despised that hideous woman. Lilbit made her return to the pink house. It was her refuge, her sanctuary, and her place of solitude.

Those under her radar that night might not have understood or agreed with the "interference," but they dared not challenge or question her "position." I have evolved in my understanding of my grandmother's stance. Lilbet simply wanted peace in the home that housed her grandbabies. She demanded there be peace and her five-foot-four-inch stature would rise to match the level of anyone threatening the homeostasis of those most precious to her. This interference played out time and time again. Lilbit was small in stature, but she was a giant as it pertained to the level of courage she housed.

Before arriving at the age of ten, I bore witness to the power housed in being courageous. I digested the power housed in being a frontline warrior for your family. I carry the ingrained example Lilbit left in my heart and it lives within my soul.

Lilbit

She was Brilliant.

She was Brave.

She was Courageous.

She was Loving.

She was Thoughtful.

She was Loyal.

She was Spiritual.

She possessed Spunk.

She possessed Sassiness.

She extended Kindness.

She extended Empathy.

She was an Overcomer.

She was a Gift.

        She was my Best Friend

        She was my Grandmother

            "Lilbit"

Chapter 4

"Unspoken Understanding"

Chapter 4

During my writing process, I reached out to my mother's youngest sibling, Aunt Debra. I shared with her the premise of my book and also explained to Auntie the impact her mother had on my existence. It was important that she understood the depth of this relationship. I'm certain that Auntie fully understood what could not be denied or minimized.

I was ten years of age when Lilbit passed. Yet, the lessons and rituals she gifted me continue to sustain me on numerous levels. How could she have impacted my life so profoundly in ten short years? Most perplexing is when I reflect on the time shared. I don't recall extensive verbal communication exchanged. I don't hold memories of Grandmother and me engaging in extensive verbal conversation. I believe there existed an unspoken understanding between Mary Elizabeth Conley and Mary Elizabeth Wilson. These are the words I expressed to Aunt Debra. I hold no memories of being yelled at or spanked. I remember there were expectations, but I do not recall extensive verbal instruction.

"Wash your hands and your face for breakfast, lunch, and dinner."

"Get to the table. It's homework time."

"It's time for school with your aunt Debra."

"Say your blessing."

"Say your prayers."

"This is appropriate."

"This is not appropriate."

It was during her subtleness with me that an understanding dwelled. I understood all she needed to deliver. I received, digested, and stored the information. I find it bewildering how many people hold the belief that information is only communicable verbally, when, in fact, nonverbal communication is just as indispensable. The receiver has to be in tune with the nonverbal cues and deliverance and hold the ability to process and place received information in its proper reference. Yes, a beautiful understanding existed between Lilbit and her granddaughter.

Chapter 5
"Gifted the Lessons by Her Actions"

Chapter 5

Grandmother prepared breakfast, lunch, and dinner daily. During my many visits to the pink house, I would sit at the kitchen table and watch as she prepared every meal. I don't recall much conversation transpiring. I sat and observed as she created culinary magic. I believe cooking was one of her many ministries. I would be quiet, not extending interruption, while absorbing every ingredient she pardoned from the pantry. She used these treasured ingredients to create magic, awakening the most trained palette.

I have decided to share with my readers a few of her recipes, as well as my favorite dishes. She did not use measurements. I am led by my taste buds. I know how each dish should taste.

RECIPES

Carrot Salad

- Shredded Carrots
- Raisins
- Diced Pineapple
- Salad Dressing

Yams

- Yams
- White Sugar
- Brown Sugar
- Walnuts (roasted)
- Caramelized Orange Peel
- Nutmeg
- Cinnamon
- Vanilla
- Butter

Mustard Greens

- Salt Pork
- Fresh Mustard Greens
- Garlic Powder
- Black Pepper
- Turnips
- Okra

Some of Lilbit's Treasured Meal Combinations

Dinner:

- Spaghetti
- Coleslaw
- Cornbread
- Kool-Aid
- (Jello with Fruit Cocktail)

Dinner:

- Roasted Pork chops
- Mustard Greens
- Peas / Rice
- Cornbread
- (Carnation Vanilla Ice Cream)

Lunch:
- Peanut Butter Sandwich
- Red Apple
- Lays Potato Chips
- Mothers Cookies
- Glass of Ice-Cold Milk

Lunch:
- Beef Bologna and Cheese Sandwich
- Orange Slices
- Lays Potato Chips
- Mothers Cookies
- Glass of Ice-Cold Milk

Breakfast:
- Cereal – Special K, Corn Flakes, or Chex
- Toast
- Slice of Fruit
- Grits
- Thick Smoked Bacon
- Eggs Sunny Side Up
- Biscuits with Butter and Strawberry Preserves
- Glass of Ice-Cold Milk

However simplistic, this is an example of how she gifted the lessons by her actions more so than by her words. As I employ more reflection, I'm reminded of how the early 1970s represented a time of rigid values and beliefs as they pertained to children and their alignment with adults:

- Very few questions were asked.
- Children were not invited to engage in adult conversation.
- Children were expected to stay in their place, lane, and zone.

As I've stated, my youngest aunt, who is just five years older than my eldest sibling, states that she recalls an in-depth conversation being shared between Grandmother and me. However, I can't recall those extensive verbal exchanges.

Chapter 6
"Her Challenges"

Chapter 6

I felt Lilbit was perfect. I know we are all simply a work in progress, and I believe that inner growth is a continuous process. However, Lilbit represented perfection. She was perfect to me on every level. I would like to think that by the time her three grandchildren arrived, she had overcome many of the challenges my mother shared; or perhaps she simply did not allow for them to impact the relationship she treasured with Richard, Russell, and me.

Lilbit was the eldest of three children and was born in 1922 to a single-parent household in Louisiana. This is the only historical information provided to me by my mother, stating:

"Liz, my mother was very private. She shared nothing with me pertaining to her life as a child, teen, young adult, or adult. She shared nothing. I knew that my mother loved me. I knew that she loved me deeply. However, I found it perplexing that she never shared with me information pertaining to her upbringing. No information shared about her father, her mother, siblings, or information about her first husband, my father.

No information shared about her sorrows, pain, regrets, hopes, or her dreams. However, the impact of her sorrows dwelled within our family home. What I learned about my mother's journey came from your great-grandmother, Liller Lewis, the child of two slaves. She was transparent, unapologetic, and displayed enthusiasm when speaking of her own journey."

My mother stated that the impact of her mother's disappointments was exhibited in her moments of sadness before the birth of her grandchildren.

Perhaps our births provided her with solitude and healing

from past disappointments or confirmation that her life had a renewed purpose. Perhaps the birth of her grandchildren provided her a love that came with no conditions attached or explanations required. The only expectations warranted were for the love and protection that she could deliver. That she did deliver.

Chapter 7
"Religious Foundation"

Chapter 7

Lilbit had a strong religious foundation. As a child, my siblings and I attended The Kingdom Hall of Jehovah's Witnesses faithfully. We participated in Saturday morning field service that included going door to door. That presented me with anxiety because we never knew what to expect. Sometimes we received a welcoming smile and, on rare occasions, we had the door slammed in our faces. Regardless of the outcome, Richard, Russell, and I were there in participation by Lilbit's side. Every Sunday morning was reserved for the Kingdom Hall. Lilbit's grandbabies, dressed to perfection, sat quietly. Lilbit never had to pull out a hairbrush, comb, ruler, or a threat. My siblings and I understood the Kingdom Hall decorum.

Did I mention the depth of my boredom? I understood nothing being stated. There I sat, chewing my gum and sucking on multi-color Life Savers, one after another, as I watched the minutes on the clock slowly tick by. As a child, Sunday service provided me with a sense of belonging and acceptance because of the smiles and embraces I received. The congregation she attended was diverse and members addressed each other as brother or sister. Lilbit was addressed as Sister Conley.

Field service on Saturday, church on Sunday, and Bible study on Wednesday. Lilbit was dedicated. I feel confident in embracing that dedication. That was my observation. However, I also observed her "struggles."

One Saturday morning, I watched cartoons while Lilbit participated in her Saturday cleaning rituals. Several of the sisters were in the community, and heading toward the pink house. Lilbit quickly disposed of her cigarette and began spraying the house. For some reason that stuck with me. I always knew my grandmother to be a smoker. As I reflect, I'm unsure if she shared her struggle to overcome this addiction with her congregation. If she had, was support and compassion extended? Just a thought.

Chapter 8

"The Embracement of Her Name—Go Figure"

Chapter 8

Mary Elizabeth (Liz), Mary Elizabeth (Liz),
Mary Elizabeth (Liz), Mary Elizabeth (Liz),
Mary Elizabeth (Liz), Mary Elizabeth (Liz)
Mary Elizbeth (Liz), Mary Elizabeth (Liz),
Mary Elizabeth (Liz), Mary Elizbeth (Liz),

As a child, I loathed my birth name. I was going to use the word hate, but felt as though it was too harsh, even though it best represents my stance. Continuously, I thought,

"Where did this name come from? Was my mother out of her mind for tagging me with this (old lady) name?" That was how my eight-year-old self felt. My classmates had cute names such as Lori, Katie, Kelli, Sandra, Tonya, Staci, Traci, Sabrina, etc.

Outside of my home, people called me Mary. Inside my home and among family, I was Liz, and this continues to this day. As a pre-teen, I was most bothered by being addressed as "Mary." Mary was such a big name for a child. Carrying such a big name was exhausting. I felt so exhausted. I assumed there was an unspoken responsibility attached to Mary Elizabeth; a rush to adulthood, and it wasn't fair. I just knew that being attached to something cute and sassy would have come with less of a responsibility. I needed to not carry that internal weight. I needed a simplified existence. In elementary school, I demanded simplicity. Go figure!

It was in high school when I embraced my name and the reality that I carried the name of my hero. The name felt heavy during my childhood because it is a big name. As stated previously, my family and close friends referred to me as Liz—carefree, easygoing, fun, and flexible. In business and outside of the home, I'm addressed as Mary—focused, business-minded, persistent, and solid.

At some point in my journey, I embraced the two, making the connection. I understood it was a blessing to carry my grandmother's name. When I comprehended that reality, I became overwhelmed, yet my heart swelled with pride, and my soul was ignited with an indescribable energy and gratitude.

I have first and second cousins who were born following Lilbit's passing. They never met her and I carry her name. A name that I had to grow into. I feel so very honored, so very blessed, and appreciative to represent her legacy—a legacy she ordained. My mother recently stated, "Liz, my mother told me to name you after her. It wasn't a request, it was an order, and I gladly obliged. At the hospital, her heart was filled with pride. She was in love the moment she saw you, her namesake: Mary Elizebeth (Liz)."

Power Housed in a Name

"Go Figure"

During my late twenties, my aunt gave birth to twins: a boy and a girl. The boy was named "Zar." At the time I thought he should have been named a trendier name such as

Justin, Ryan, Jacob, Dillon, etc, but his father stated, "I want my son to have the name of a warrior. He is going to be named Zar." I thought to myself, *That is no name for a baby. This is not okay. Why is my aunt allowing this?* Thirty-four years later, Zar has grown into a handsome, strong, kind, intelligent human. He is a loving husband, father, and friend. Zar is courageous, brave, intelligent, and a warrior for humanity. His name is perfect, representing all that he encompasses.

Zar had to grow into his name. For a child, I felt the name was a large weight to carry. However, I failed to understand what his parents knew to be true—his name was going to transcend beyond his childhood. As I stand with my cousin in adulthood, I marvel over his name.

What a powerful name: Zar. The name of a warrior. The name of a king.

Just like Zar, I was also given a large name at birth, a powerful name chosen to transcend into my adulthood, and that it has. Go figure!

Chapter 9

"My Badge of Shame"

Chapter 9

Aunt Debra and I shared a powerful event that will never depart from our psyches. Lilbit's last day on Earth was spent with Aunt Debra and me. We were with her hours before her earthly assignment concluded. I will share the events of that catastrophic day from both of our perspectives.

Mary Elizabeth Jr.
(Age 10)

The day my childhood changed forever began like so many days spent with my grandmother. I recall certain aspects as though it were twenty minutes ago. The feelings associated with that day are never far from my memory and the grief associated with the loss of my soulmate.

Grandmother had spent the day cleaning her home while humming the lyrics to her favorite Motown hits and addressing errands. I always felt safe at Grandmother's. I loved venturing from room to room, embracing the sense of freedom that I yearned for and needed.

At some point, Grandmother stated she was going to take a nap, and that she did. Hours later, my mother retrieved me. I did not feel the need to wake Lilbit. I knew I would return in a few days. Following my arrival at our newly purchased home on the other side of town, I would like to think Lilbit's name had been announced at morning roll call as the angels gathered to prepare for their journey to retrieve her. As death slowly made its arrival, I was in the bathroom, brushing my hair, and staring into the mirror, reminiscing about my stay at the pink house, when I heard my mother on the kitchen phone. Her tone was different. She was demanding answers to questions. "When? Where? How?" followed by lapses of silence and whispers. Then there was a gentle knock on the bathroom door. My mother opened the door with moist eyes, using the counter to support her stoic frame as she gently stated, "Liz, your grandmother passed away." She shared nothing further with me at that moment. I later gathered more details from overhearing the various conversations exchanged by the adults within the family.

Debra Conley
(Age 15)

It was a peaceful day. Mom had been cleaning, and I was in the den. She and I had made plans to go on a mother-daughter date. I had just started a new job, and I was going to celebrate by treating her to dinner. I was so excited. At some point, Dad came home from work and asked, "Where is your mom?" I told him she was taking a nap. Dad sat out on the front porch, relaxing. Eventually, he went to check on her. He called her name and there was no response. He turned her over and there was blue liquid coming from her nose and mouth. Dad phoned the paramedics.

Our cousins, who lived next door, rushed over. There was a lot of commotion coming from the bedroom. They kept me out. I tried my best to weave my small frame through the larger bodies, but they wouldn't let me in.

After what felt like hours, the bedroom door flung open, as the paramedics rushed Lilbit down the hallway, out the front door into an awaiting ambulance, and transported her to the hospital. Sometime later, I remember the living room telephone being answered by cousin Bon and observing his wife, our cousin Gwen's distraught facial expression. Dad's words projected from the phone as he mumbled, "Give chicken the phone," the nickname he bestowed upon me. My emotions were imprisoned by the elevated beating of my heart. Dad was crying as he stated, "I'm so sorry. I'm so sorry. I am so sorry. I don't know how to finish raising you."

I fell to the floor, screaming and crying. I felt numb and lost. I never thought about my parents dying. I had the sense to know that they would, but life was so good. My parents were so cute together. They shared Sunday afternoon drives, dinner dates, and shopping. My mother loved my father, and he adored her. Dad was the provider. He worked and handed the check to her. That is what he believed to be his purpose. He felt pride in that role. Mom worked for Ms. McKintosh two days a week and she loved that independence, but Dad was proud to be the provider and that he was.

Mary Elizabeth Jr.

I was consumed with mounting guilt. Guilt manifesting from a heinous act I willfully participated in. Weeks before my grandmother's death, I was engaging with a group of neighborhood friends, in a challenge to determine who was brave enough to say, "Bloody Mary, bloody Mary" in the dark, facing a mirror and stand fearless to face the outcome—an outcome representing something devastating. That was the challenge.

In the days following the dare, I clearly remember walking into my hallway bathroom, turning off the light, staring into the darkness, unable to recognize the features before me. My breathing accelerated as my chest expanded, providing a release of the forbidden words, "Bloody Mary, bloody Mary, bloody Mary." I repeated with increased acceleration to show them I had courage and I wasn't scared. I was ten years old, and I was brave. Weeks following my grandmother's passing, immediately I was overwhelmed with guilt that pierced my soul. I carried that guilt throughout my childhood. It was my badge of shame. On some level, I felt responsible for Lilbit's death. I had caused her name to be placed on the morning roll call list. It was all my fault. If I knew nothing else, I owned that truth.

Debra Conley
(Age 15)

"I felt as though this could not be real. I was crushed, scared, unsure, and alone (because we were so close). I needed my mom. Who could I confide in? Who could I trust, who would have my back? Being a young lady? I had just started dating. Who would provide guidance? I did not know what to expect, not being able to see her, hug her, or spend time with her. I felt empty and as time went on, I remember being able to hear her voice in my head, recalling things she would say, and her laugh that gave me comfort. As time passed, I would think about her, but I could no longer hear her voice. That freaked me out. I remember stating, "Have I forgotten about her?" It was difficult, but the family love and encouragement kept me strong."

CHAPTER 10

"The Birth of a Shift"

Chapter 10

Following a short reprieve, my mother, my siblings, and I, along with my guilt, arrived at the pink house. For the next several days, family, neighbors, and friends stopped by to extend their condolences, deliver savory dishes, hugs and kisses, laughter, heightened storytelling, and assist with funeral preparations—all a welcomed distraction, momentarily achieving their goal. Before the stately black hearse made its grand entrance through the silver gates, I forgot my Lilbit had transitioned, and from the whaling and screams, most had also disassociated from that reality.

I remember the service being held at the Kingdom Hall. I sat in silence, staring off into the far distance, avoiding contact with the metal that imprisoned her body. There I sat, not feeling much of anything. There was no chewing of gum or sucking on multicolor Life Savers to soothe my broken spirit. I will never forget the viewing of my grandmother's body. The navy blue and white dress her daughters selected was beautiful. Lilbit's black wavy hair was combed in an unfamiliar style. I was struck by the absence of her beautiful French bun. Her hair was mesmerizing. Each short curl was elegantly positioned. Despite my sorrow housed in her death, Lilbit remained a vision of beauty. The fullness of her lips adorned the trademark "apple red" lipstick. Grandmother looked as beautiful as ever. I'm grateful that my memory of that day is of my soulmate looking the way she always had. Her long black eyelashes gently laid against her silky auburn skin. She looked to be at peace; simply taking an afternoon rest to soothe her spirit. That was an appropriate way for me to remember her on that day. Being only ten, anything of the unfamiliar would have only added to the suffrage awaiting me.

The grave site service was tranquil. I found myself

worrying about my middle aunt, Rushell. She was married and pregnant with her first child. Unbeknownst to me, my ten-year-old self wanted to protect her from the anguish that day represented. Her husband, a church elder, stood dutifully by her side, but I wanted to ensure that she received additional care and shielding. My mother was prideful in her position as eldest, ensuring the service flowed properly. Several years later, Mom shared how she perfected the art of masking her pain and how this attribute provided her internal refuge. Mom secured her mask and extended love and support to others, which included checking in on my grandfather.

Russell Conley (Wee) was a stoic man, never one to display a collection of emotion or open affection. He prided himself on doing what was perceived as doing right. Without failure, he was the provider his family could depend on. On that day, Grandpa was without words and appeared to be in a state of reflection. Perhaps, pondering on what was next now that his queen had transitioned. What would be the expectation? Perhaps that was his thought.

"My mother often shared how Russell Conley was a man of honor. Even though he expressed few words, his actions spoke

volumes as they pertained to the love he reserved for his wife, children, and grandchildren. Grandpa was proudly employed by the City of San Diego Department of Parks and Recreation and on one occasion that represented many, Mom stated that his work boots had ripped open, so Grandpa had wrapped his boots with black duct tape. Grandmother felt that this was not okay and insisted he purchase new work boots. Grandpa replied, "I'm fine. I want to make sure you all have what you need. You and the children are my priority. I'm just fine."

That was the man Lilbit married. Every time I revisit that memory, my eyes well up and my heart overflows with emotion. Grandpa was amazing.

Following the graveside service, family and friends returned to grandmother's home. I remember lots of people, lots of conversation, and delicious food—the usual "repast" spread, but this was heightened deliciousness: fried chicken, roast beef, ham, potato salad, green beans, yams, collard greens, cabbage, macaroni & cheese, cornbread, rolls, and a spread of desserts, along with punch, tea, and grandmother's favorite: Folgers coffee.

The house echoed with forced laughter as the adults shared treasured memories. Lost in my own little chaotic world, I sat in silence. Within this realm of silence, I felt the manifestation of a shift being birthed and there was nothing I could do to alter the impact it would have on my journey. There would be no more trips to Sawaya Brothers, no more cooking demonstrations, no more housekeeping trips, no more visitations at Ragsdale Funeral Home, and no more requests for me to be Lilbit's plus one. No more *Young and the Restless*, *Guiding Light*, *General Hospital*, or *As the World Turns*. No more Lilbit's mustard greens, pork chops, spaghetti, fried chicken, chop suey, or carrot salad. No more Jello with fruit cocktail or Carnation vanilla ice cream. No more of her eggs sunny side up, pancakes, or thick bacon from the butcher.

Lilbit was in heaven, at peace, rejoicing with the angels, and I was left behind. She never left me. Even when I protested to be left, she never left me. However, on the day her assigned angels arrived to bring her home, Lilbit left me behind and my world would never be the same.

Chapter 11

"Change"

Chapter 11

As time passed, there were fewer visitors, fewer delivered meals, fewer phone calls, and a decrease in the receiving of cards, notes, and letters. A period of time passed before I visited my grandmother's home, and that was just fine with me. We had inherited her dog, Tuffy. She loved that dog. He was her baby. It did not feel appropriate to have Tuffy at our home, as it was a daily reminder of her absence. Tuffy had been an indoor dog and at our home, he was not allowed to stay indoors... "change." To the best of her ability, Grandmother ensured the peace, making sure there was a sense of order... "change." The biggest change and impact on my emotional well-being I experienced was during a visit to the pink house following her death. As my mother's teal Dodge Charger made its way through the haggard silver gates and turned into the driveway, nervousness and intense anxiety consumed every inch of my ten-year-old frame. It was early afternoon, yet the pink house appeared dreary. As we approached the front door, no jasmine or gardenia aroused my senses or savory aromas welcoming my siblings and me. Instead, dreariness and glumness welcomed us. Everything looked sad—the carpet, curtains, sofa, and chair. Even the paintings reflected a sadness. The warmth, laughter, and Joy—gone.

As I entered the kitchen, there was no trace of my soulmate. Her white stove, refrigerator, coffee pot, toaster, and blender were there, but no Lilbet. I guess I expected her to suddenly appear. That had been my daily prayer. I felt her energy nowhere.

The bed she took her last breath in was there, but no Lilbit. Her dresses, white tennis shoes, and nightgowns were there, but no Lilbit. Her treasured perfume and favorite apple red lipstick sat where she last placed them on her gold vanity. There they all remained, but no Lilbit. However, what was present was fear. The heartbeat of the home that had been my wonderland, my refuge, my solitude, my safety net, my everything—gone. There was no trace of what was. No trace of what I needed to thrive. It had vanished, replaced with uncertainty. I took a deep breath to lessen the queasiness and yet another to protect my sanity. I was anxiety-ridden. I found the closet corner and nestled my ten-year-old frame into every available inch. I needed a protector and the wooden crevices filled that need. My friend was gone and her home felt like a morgue.

As the months passed, Grandpa became more subdued, navigating in silence. Losing her mother at fifteen traumatized my youngest aunt. She was angry, uncertain of her future, and filled with grief. Losing your mom at fifteen wasn't fair. Something didn't feel right about saying goodbye to your mom at fifteen.

As time passed, I spent less time at the pink house. All the joy and excitement visits embodied before Lilbit's death were absent. I'm grateful that my mom never pressured me to visit. My pain and grief would be extensive. Perhaps Mom finally understood a fragment of my suffrage.

Aunt Debra spent time at our home, and that suited me just fine. Mom embraced a motherly position with her younger sister. My siblings and I loved when she spent time at our home. She had always been an important figure in our childhood. Lilbit depended on her during the time spent at the pink house to assist with various tasks that pertained to the grandchildren, and Auntie embraced those responsibilities.

From time to time, we would participate in family dinners at the pink house, definitely a rarity. Truth be told, the day my best friend took her last breath, my relationship with the pink house concluded. I was done. Pink was just another color.

Chapter 12

"Traumatized (Inner Bully)"

Chapter 12

Before Lilbit's death, teachers regarded me as a well-behaved fourth grader whose only sin as it pertained to school was talking excessively in class. As a young thriving Aquarius, I embraced my analytical skills, and boy, did I love expressing my thoughts. Regardless of gender, ethnicity, culture, or status, all classmates were open prey as it pertained to the sharing of my perspectives. I discussed my favorite school subjects: English, reading, writing, math, and history.

I debated sports" football, kickball, softball, and track and field. I shared my love of dance, shopping, sleepovers, baking, and creative writing. I provided the 411 on what was being served in the cafeteria daily and debated which entrée was the tastiest: tacos, lasagna, enchiladas, hot dogs, or meatloaf. I also celebrated my cafeteria favorites: mashed potatoes topped with chunks of turkey breast and white gravy; savory meatloaf with bits of onion and bell pepper smothered in rich brown gravy; crispy tacos stuffed with ground beef, lettuce, tomatoes, and cheese. Each bite left my lips smeared with Crisco lip gloss. I discussed my love for The Jackson Five, The Osmonds, The Sylvers, Sonny and Cher, the DeBarge Family, and *Right On!* magazine. I cried to my friend Cynthia about my breasts not arriving and how I wanted to purchase a training bra. That was my number one priority.

The fact that I was deprived of that rite of passage as a fourth grader wasn't fair. I demanded vindication. As an inquisitive fifth grader, I talked about not getting my menstrual cycle and how others got theirs. I prayed to God and reminded him of my growing impatience. I bragged to all about my love for my classmate Richard Conde and his resemblance to my adult crush, Bruce Lee.

Every report card noted "excessive talking." At every parent-teacher conference, my teacher stressed to my mother that it was important that I maintain "compliance" during class instruction. They deemed me as extremely bright, and I prided myself on the embracement of that truth. I loved sharing my various perspectives, and nothing was off-limits except the death of my best friend. There would be no revisiting that—EVER!

Following Lilbet's death, there was a shift. My protector was gone. The person who ensured balance and accountability within her family system was gone. The person who made my heart smile was gone and, from my perspective, my world was falling apart. I did not look angry, but my actions represented a behavior that was of concern. I had a disagreement with a classmate whom I considered a close friend. I attacked her. I attacked my friend. Our parents demanded that we resolve the issue. We never mended the friendship.

I was angry and filled with rage, capitalizing on a misunderstanding or a threat that would have been previously ignored, providing me an excuse to unload the grief and pain I was harboring. On occasion, I would provide my unloading services free of charge to those under attack. I became a self-proclaimed Robin Hood of Audubon Elementary School. A younger student approached me and asked if I could provide protection. She stated that an older student had threatened to beat her up after school. I took on this assignment and handled the situation. You best believe I did.

I went from wearing dresses to rocking blue jeans, black Converse, and tee shirts with my windbreaker tied around my waist. I stayed ready so there would be no need to get ready. I never knew when a situation would present itself; when I would be called upon to defend a student in distress. I needed to be prepared and prepared I was.

In 2011, *Redbook* magazine featured an article highlighting women who were overcomers. It was during their interview process and much internal reflection that I came to understand that my bullying behavior presented following Lilbit's passing. The realization prompted me to pull back more layers. What I discovered was life-altering. You see, when my grandmother passed on the day my mother told me of her passing, no one provided instructions to my ten-year-old self on how to process the devastating information. She simply delivered it, and that was it.

Immediately, the family went into planning mode. From my young eyes, everyone appeared consumed with their loss, their pain, their sorrow, and eventually their healing. I don't recall being asked, "Liz, how are you doing?" or "How are you coping?" or "Liz, how has this loss impacted you?" My best friend died, and no one checked on me. Had someone, anyone, reached out to me on a deeper level, perhaps they would have recognized the trauma I endured, the pain in my soul, the anger I embodied, and eventually the rage brewing.

People think children cannot internalize pain. Many fail to recognize children grieve a loss and their suffering is profound. I unleashed my unaddressed anger and rage on my classmates. Within our family home, my parents had zero tolerance for disobedience, so the only safe place for me to unleash my pain was on the school grounds.

Inside the classroom, I continued to present myself as a model student except for the excessive "sharing of my thoughts." At home, I was a model child. However, deep within, I was suffering from a horrific loss, one that was debilitating. I had to lighten this load. I had to lessen the pain. These emotions were consuming me on every level. I no longer recognized myself. Plagued with anxiety, my existence became a distortion of a past I yearned for.

Emotional detachment was my cure; a prescription that proved to be the least effective. I was wetting my bed nightly. I can't recollect when this behavior manifested. I recall the shame and guilt. As if that wasn't enough, punishment was the recommended prescription to cure "laziness." The antidote for a fifth grader who was too lazy to get out of bed and use the restroom. I devised the perfect plan to produce success. I would deprive myself of: liquids hours before bedtime, sleep by pacing the floors all night, and rest by reading my favorite books before falling asleep. This plan of action proved to be a game of war between my psyche and my bladder. On many nights I was the victor, waking from my sleep, throwing the covers back, and rushing to the bathroom with Olympic speed, making it to the toilet. There I sat as the warmth streamed from my body and onto my sheets. I lay in a pool of urine, overcome with shame and guilt as I awaited the consequences. This night was reflective of so many.

My suffering caused me to endure additional distress because of the adults in my life's inability to recognize the impact of my trauma; no conversations addressing my status, no therapy sessions, or assessments. I somehow navigated through my pain using denial, displacement, and projection. The source of my perceived delinquencies remained unresolved. Categorized as "the bully," I embraced that label, a label that defined who and what I had become. In the mind of a traumatized sixth grader, there was no other logical explanation.

In time, my anger decreased. However, I continued to identify as the tough kid, the one not to cross, the one whose friends were never to be crossed, and the one who fought the battles of those unable to defend themselves. The one they could depend on and that they did. Following many months of self-employment, I became bored. This occupation became tiring. I was exhausted and ready for a radical transformation.

Chapter 13

"Metamorphosis (Outside In)"

Chapter 13

As I prepared to enroll in the seventh grade, I became overwhelmed with racing thoughts as there were three decisions before me: 1) Continue as a tough kid and face the tougher kids in junior high school, 2) Do nothing and let fate decide my destiny, or 3) Transform myself from the outside in.

There were older girls in the neighborhood known for being brave, well respected, sassy, classy, confident, and intelligent. Out of desperation and mounting fear of getting my butt kicked, I made the decision to transform myself into a young lady who embodied many of the attributes of the young ladies I admired. I envisioned exuding kindness, compassion, generosity, increased intelligence, empathy, courage, and faith. That was my goal. Initially, I was unsure how to achieve this plight. I had to begin somewhere, so I started with addressing my exterior. I changed my hairstyle to something more inviting. The ponytails were out, and long curls were in. I trashed my black and white Converse, jeans, masculine shirts, and the blue windbreaker with the broken zipper. I loved having that jacket secured around my skinny waist every day. That had been my trademark, my armor, and now it was being relieved of duty.

I reported to the seventh grade wearing a dress, sandals, bracelets, earrings, and my lips glistening with lip gloss. I had my hair pressed, curled, and flowing down my back. I was ready on every level. Before I knew or understood the power housed in vision boards and affirmations, I was making use of them as constant reminders. Before I understood cognitive therapy, I was employing this therapeutic intervention:

Liz, you are smart
You are kind
You are loving

You are beautiful
You are amazing
You are brave
You are not your past
You are an overcomer
You are courageous

In addition, I was purposeful in my goal to elevate others with words of encouragement. Daily, I found ways in which to acknowledge and pour into others. I simply found joy in highlighting the attributes I saw in my fellow peers. I embraced this mission without a clear understanding of the impact these actions would have on my growth. As my internal elevation soared, all the kindness and positive energy I planted into the universe was being reciprocated. My soul was being watered. I was growing. I was flourishing. Most importantly, I was healing. The unaddressed wounds from my grandmother's death were healing. As my healing process accelerated, I found within myself the courage to confront my grief. At the age of fourteen, I found within myself the ability to hope for a positive future representing a young lady that would make my grandmother proud.

Chapter 14

"Time Brings About Change"

Chapter 14

For better or for worse, time brings about change, and as the years passed, my youngest aunt married and started a family of her own. My middle aunt had two additional children. My aunt Diane, just two years younger than my mother, gave birth to three sons before passing away in 1989. Following years of suffering, my grandfather remarried. Even though no one could ever replace the spirit of Lilbet, the new Mrs. Conley was loving and kind. Grandfather maintained his commitment to our family. He never wavered from his belief as it pertained to his position and all responsibilities. I found within myself the ability to cope with my new normal. I discovered a sense of peace and purpose as I navigated through life without Lilbet.

Eventually, I married, gave birth to two courageous daughters, and was blessed with a loving bonus son. As a military dependent, I traveled throughout the United States with the U.S. Navy. That was a rich experience. Embracing people from different ethnicities and cultures was a powerful gift to bestow upon my children. After completing my education, I became a licensed clinical therapist (LCSW) and served as a Juvenile Justice Commissioner for eight years. Then I received instruction to move to Houston, Texas, to embrace my next earthly assignment.

With each passing year, I have evolved on every level. I never stopped growing, I never stopped evolving, and as I grew, the lessons my grandmother gifted were never far from my remembrance. They have maintained a powerful presence, dwelling on a cellular level, and guiding my daily existence.

Recipes: Her recipes have provided succulent nourishment to my family, godchildren, and friends during Sunday dinners and holiday celebrations.

Gift of Giving: It is because of my observing Lilbet's gift of giving, I embrace her level of giving. In doing so, whenever a child departs from my home, I gift them a departing treat. My adult children and their friends also are benefactors of Lilbit's giving spirit.

Loving Spirit: Lilbit was a remarkable wife, mother, grandmother, and friend. She loved us all deeply. Each of my siblings felt as though we were her favorite. Her love had no limits. Love is the foundation of all I have mentioned thus far. I, like Lilbit, am in love with love. I understand that love is the foundation and there is no greater investment. Lilbit invested in love, as do I.

Compassionate: Lilbit's level of compassion inspired me to give of myself by checking in on others. I don't do the funeral thing, but I visit those who have passed in prayer and meditation. I speak with Lilbit daily as I seek her continued guidance. I check in on the living by sending cards, letters, emails, and text messages. As I celebrate myself, I find joy in celebrating others. I find contentment in doing so. I stand on the frontline for humanity, living my life and making a difference by embodying the lessons that have sustained me.

Chapter 15

"A Grandmother's Love Transcends"

Chapter 15

I don't recall the date or the time, but at some point, I grew into this large name. It was as though one day I made the connection. I came to understand Mary Elizebeth was the name of Lilbit. How did this information go unprocessed? Before her death, she was Lilbit, Liz, Grandmother, or Momma. I don't remember her being referred to as Mary Elizebeth.

My mother shared that before my birth, Lilbit blatantly stated, "If it's a girl, she is going to have my name." My mother stated that was a command not to be challenged. Lilbit gifted her greatest gift to me. I embraced my understanding of that truth and at that moment of embracement, I also grasped the significance of the moment. It was an awakening that led to an internal release. Tears overflowed as an acknowledgment of that gift. I received the gift of the name of a woman who meant everything to me.

At this moment, as I sit noting my thoughts, I'm present as it pertains to my comprehension and the emotions associated. My grandmother lives within my soul twenty-four-seven. My external embodiment does not go unnoticed. On my lips, I wear her trademark apple red lipstick. I pop my gum in a manner that reminds my mother of her mom. I'm sassy, confident, bold, classy, and "BRAVE" just like my Lilbit. Most importantly, I share her loving nature, her level of compassion, and her giving spirit.

Every time I'm addressed by my birth name, the place within my heart reserved for her awakens. Her essence dwells within, reminding me of her earthly journey. I'm reminded of her existence. I'm also reminded of her rituals, her level of faith, her giving spirit, and how deeply she loved. I will never forget her earthly visit. I will never forget my LILBIT.

GREATEST LESSONS GIFTED BY YOUR GRANDMOTHER

"Love deeply but never depend on a man for sustainment. Work hard and always have your own"

– MarShana Gilder

"Surround yourself with people who treat you with respect and don't wait until you're trying to get into heaven to be kind."

–Lora Kent

"The biggest lesson I learned from my grandmother is faith. She instilled faith in me. She, along with my mother, laid the foundation for my faith in God."

–Anthony Regiv

"My grandmother taught me the importance of being kind, extending kindness without expecting anything in return."

–Yvonne Hollis

"My grandmother was the greatest after my mom. She taught us respect, honesty, and unconditional love. She was always there for us."

–Bettye Wright

"No matter what we go through, we are family."

–Danerien

"No matter how rich or how poor you are, all a baby needs is love."

–Danerien

"To love yourself, no matter what."

–Rhonda Bland

"Interacting with my grandmother taught me strength, determination, to have my own mindset, not to fall into concentrating on what other people thought of me (being my own person), and not to be ashamed of falling short in life. She was a courageous woman, who was also feisty. It's been an honor to be brought up in a family, from my mom to my father, and grandmother."

–Lillian Norris

"My grandmothers were God-fearing, strong, confident, classy, and giving women. They knew what they wanted and gave no apologies for it. That's the gift they extended to me."

–Geralyn Moseley

"My grandmother taught me that God is far more loving, more accepting, and less critical than man. He created you to be uniquely you. Live to please Him only and do so unapologetically."

–Kiesha Curtis-Baker

"When people hurt and do harm, they have to answer to God. That's what Big Momma taught me."

–Danny Sneed

"To appreciate the freedom we have just by being born in America."

–Rebecca Bowen

"A hand too closed to give will never receive. Selfishness alone, you may be fragile but together you are unbreakable."

–Simone Utsey

"My grandmothers are the type of women who are always on the positive side of things. When they set their minds to something, they don't stray in order to get it done. They both have taught me the value of staying positive and focused."

–Richard Russell, Jr.

"My great-grandmother told me that you teach people how to treat you. So love yourself."

–Wonder Trotter

"When your husband asks you to go somewhere, never say no. You go. Enjoy that treasured time with him."

–Zela Ocon

"What Your Grandmother Meant to You"

Greg Fulton

"My grandmother was called "Big Momma." She was my joy, my love, and my peace. Big Momma stayed down the street from us in the city of Memphis, Tennesee.

Big Momma died on August 16, 1969. I was ten years old. Big Momma helped shape my life at an early age. Although we lived three houses down the street from her, when we went down to Big Momma's, it was like a vacation away from home. Big Momma inspired me to show love to others and to share peace and joy with others. I remember Big Momma talking to me and following I would feel like "Superman." She was the Big Momma of the neighborhood. She was my everything.

At age 62, I can still remember the seeds of love, peace, and joy that Big Momma planted in my life at age ten. That was over fifty years ago. I love and miss you, Big Momma.

Your grandson, Greg."

Adrienne Sierra

"My nanna meant the world to me. She was a proud American. She immigrated here from Spain and was poorly educated. She desperately wanted to be a citizen, but knew she couldn't pass the test. She promised to be a proud American, to respect the laws of this country, and to vote in every election. They granted her citizenship, and she lived up to her promises until the day she died!"

Terri Glave

"She was the queen of the hill in my eyes, my grandmother Leona Turner. I affectionally called her Momma, as she was like a second mom to me and I was more like a daughter to her.

She instilled in me the love of our God, pride, to have my own, time, money, and friends. She also shared with me the importance of loving unconditionally. She taught me so much, but most of all, she taught me how to be a wife and grandmother.

Gladys Castillo

"Unfortunately, I did not have the pleasure of meeting either of my grandmothers. They both passed away before I was born. From my mother's stories, I learned from my grandmother to be strong and assertive, a protective mother, productive, and business savvy.

From my paternal grandmother, I learned the importance of prayer and faith. She gave birth to sixteen children. My father was her fifteenth child. Not only was she extremely resilient, my father spoke of her deep devotion to prayer. When my father unexpectedly lost his eyesight as a young boy, he remembered how his mother would walk to church and pray so fervently every morning at sunrise for several months. One morning, his eyesight was mysteriously and miraculously restored. He strongly believed it was because of his mother's prayers and her unwavering faith. My father became a successful criminal attorney in Manila."

Suanne Grayson

"Since losing my grandmother, I realize that I should have devoted more time to listening to her stories. She was a first-generation American and had unique experiences. I am dedicating myself to locate my extended family that I have never met to tell them what a great person she was."

Sandra Atwaters

"My grandmother, known as Big Momma, was a very wise woman and a nurse. She always reminded me to treat people with kindness and the way I would want to be treated. She wore her heart on her sleeve. I also remember her telling me, while in the kitchen cooking with her, "Peaches (my nickname), make sure you know how to cook for yourself or your future husband. May she rest in heaven. I love you, Big Momma."

Lillian Norris

"I would say the relationship with my grandmother (Liller Lewis) was a good and positive relationship. I remember the first contact I had with my grandmother was by phone. Not sure how often we (grandchildren) conversed with her in a year, I would say every couple of months. She had a great sense of humor; she was loving, proud, strong, and strong-willed. I remember talking with her on the phone around the age of five years old. She would remind me to always listen to my parents, keep my dress down 101 (I was only five), and always let me know how much she loved and missed me. As I got older, she would talk to me and remind me to always be a great student and never take for granted my education (because she could not read or write)."

Tiera Cornish

"For me my Granny means countless moments of laughter, the best homemade pound cake and popcorn. Comforting foot rubs, long talks about life lessons, cha cha dancing in the living room, rolled tacos with wine, listening to Biggie Smalls on road trips to Los Angeles, and being silly which only leads to more laughter. I feel so fortunate to have a Granny who is not only the matriarch of our family but she is one of my dearest friends. She is my sunshine on any day."

DISCUSSION QUESTIONS

1. How were you inspired by the book?

2. What are some of the memories you hold of time shared with your grandmother?

3. Which chapter was your favorite?

4. What one word describes the impact Liz and Lilbit's journey had on you?

5. What was the most profound incident that occurred in the book from your perspective?

6. What are your thoughts on the author's creativity and depth in telling the journey of Liz and Lilbit? Could you feel the various dimensions presented?

7. Please share a few of the rituals and lessons gifted to you by your grandmother.

8. How did you process the trauma Liz experienced following Lilbit's passing?

9. What are your thoughts about Liz's ability to overcome her challenges?

WORD OF HELLO

In the seventh grade, I realized that I was sent here to live my life as a writer. Regardless of any other accomplishments I may achieve, my purpose is to elevate humanity through the written word—telling stories and sharing experiences that captivate the mind and ignite the soul.

Maintaining compliance with my earthly assignment is vital. As I commit to staying aligned with my purpose, it is equally imperative that you connect with yours. Embrace your assignment and allow it to come to fruition, never forgetting the power that lies in walking in faith and obedience.

Embrace the power,
Ignite the power,
Celebrate the power housed in your existence,

–M.E.G

ABOUT THE AUTHOR

Mary was born and raised in beautiful San Diego, California. However, she shares that her spirit is most deeply connected to Northern California, particularly Sausalito. Mary is a proud graduate of Samuel Morse High School and went on to earn a master's degree from San Diego State University (SDSU).

She has spent the majority of her adult life as a frontline warrior, serving as a Licensed Clinical Social Worker (LCSW-S) and as a Commissioner. In addition to her clinical work, Mary is also a speaker, mentor, producer, and advocate for human rights.

Mary says she is most proud of maintaining compliance with her earthly assignment, which is fulfilled by inspiring the minds of those who embrace her literature.

She has successfully completed three powerful books: *A Misrepresentation of Myself* (2009), *Even a Man Can Have a Broken Heart* (2014), and *Lilbit* (2025).

Mary E. Conley
"Lilbit"

MY HEROES

All of the patients, past and present, receiving treatment at the University of Texas M.D. Anderson Cancer Center...

and

All of the patients, past and present, receiving treatment at TIRR Memorial Hermann Neurological Rehabilitation Center.

I WAS NEVER ALONE: A TRIBUTE OF THANKS

In 2017 my Life forever changed. My level of Gratitude extends to the masses however, these individuals poured into my soul as I laid in my hospital bed paralyzed at TIRR. When I could not remember my words, they made sure I maintained HOPE.

- Deryl Holden, you phoned every day for two months, reminding me of the importance of maintaining faith, courage, and hope.

- Sheryl Foreman, during my hospital stay, you spent every Sunday with me and brought lovely flower arrangements. During those visits, when I slept, you slept. You were exhausted, but you still made those Sunday visits.

- Liz Fobbs, your scripture readings kept my soul hydrated with reminders of Jehovah's unconditional love.

- Rayford Gilder, thank you for ensuring all financial needs were addressed. I had everything I needed. I'm forever grateful for that.

- Yvonne Hollis, you appointed yourself manager over the nursing staff, ensuring 24-hour spoiling. You and the girls made sure I was never alone—and I truly never was.

- Kaiden Davis, at the age of eight, you were inspired to Marco Polo me every day. I enjoyed the prayers, musical performances, readings, comedy shows, words of encouragement, and dance routines. You are a treasure.

- To my "Mary, we got you" colleagues at the Veterans Administration (VA), thank you for your weekly visits, phone calls, flowers, reading materials, and encouragement. When I graduated from TIRR Outpatient Rehab, you showed up and welcomed me back with open arms: Robert, Greg, Kiesha, Jermaine, Crystal, Amish, Carmichael, Melissa, Georgette, Liz, Tracey, Tracy, Vance, Annie, Danny, Eboni, Talley, Andrew, Dana, Detelshia, Angel, Dr. Crowley, Dr. Marsh, and Cheryl Loya.

- Tiera Cornish, thank you for being the best medical advisor. You provided advocacy, education, and leadership on every level. I will never forget the care you extended. At the end of each day, you sat bedside and provided family and friends detailed updates as it pertained to my progress.

- MarShana Gilder, thank you for ensuring that I maintained proper nutrition. You even assessed the snacks approved by my physician. I looked forward to my late-night tuna and chicken salad sandwiches—until you determined the salt levels weren't quite appropriate! I also smile when I reflect on how you were the victor of our nightly board and card games. At the time, I thought the tournament was unfair, but I later realized that, in addition to my rigorous daily rehab, you were also masterfully challenging my brain to promote neuroplasticity.

- A big thank-you is extended to: Terri Glave, Cheryl Curry, Airiel Quintana, Gladys Castillo, Tasha Radonski, Rhonda Bland, Lady Gilder, Adrienne Sierra, Cynthia Brown, the McCants Family, Toni Brundage, Kiesha Harris, Jessie Morish, Treva Felton, Carol Staton, Todd Wilson, Kristen Lim, the Russell Family, the Nelson Family, Donna Alexander, Gloria Ifil, Thelmon Jackson, Jeanette Weston, the Latchison Family, the Venegas Family, the Fulton Family, the Wallace Family, the Sneed Family, Craig Wilson, Simeon Gilder, the Houch Family, the Norris Family, Tara Hollis, Christy Hollis,

Tama Gilder, Shenitra Davis, Nichol Garvie, Geralyn Mosely, Michelle Estelle, Spencer Foreman, Christiana Foreman, Chrystne Fobbs, Eddie Fobbs, Robert Holden, Stacy Holden, Jocelyn Hobdy, Demetris Owens, Thomas Johnson, Sokum Mao, the Ocon Family, Anthony Foreman, Richard Holden, Simone Utsey, Tamu Gramby, Garrett Meier, and Felix Bilong.

CLOSING MESSAGE

I have lived courageously, loved deeply, and overcome adversity—all while embracing this truth: There is power housed in every step of my journey.

And just the same—

There is power housed in every step of *your* journey.
Never forget that truth.

Endless blessings, endless love,
M.E.G

www.ingramcontent.com/pod-product-compliance
Lightning Source LLC
Chambersburg PA
CBHW031147160426
43193CB00008B/287